Tigers

by Claire Archer

ABDO
BIG CATS
Kids

Visit us at www.abdopublishing.com

Published by Abdo Kids, a division of ABDO, P.O. Box 398166, Minneapolis, Minnesota 55439.

Copyright © 2015 by Abdo Consulting Group, Inc. International copyrights reserved in all countries. No part of this book may be reproduced in any form without written permission from the publisher.

Printed in the United States of America, North Mankato, Minnesota.

032014

092014

 PRINTED ON RECYCLED PAPER

Photo Credits: Shutterstock, Thinkstock

Production Contributors: Teddy Borth, Jennie Forsberg, Grace Hansen

Design Contributors: Dorothy Toth, Renée LaViolette, Laura Rask

Library of Congress Control Number: 2013952315

Cataloging-in-Publication Data

Archer, Claire.

Tigers / Claire Archer.

　p. cm. -- (Big cats)

ISBN 978-1-62970-006-9 (lib. bdg.)

Includes bibliographical references and index.

1. Tigers--Juvenile literature.   I. Title.

599.756--dc23

　　　　　2013952315

Table of Contents

Tigers

Tigers live throughout Asia.

The Bengal tiger is the most

common tiger. It lives in India.

Tigers live in many different **habitats**. They live in swamps, **grasslands**, and **rainforests**.

6

A tiger's stripes are like your fingerprints. No two tigers have the same stripes.

Tigers are big cats. Big cats

are the only cats that can roar.

13

Tigers are the biggest members of the cat family. They can weigh more than 650 pounds (296 kg)!

15

Food

Tigers are meat eaters. They
eat animals like deer, antelope,
and water buffalo.

Lone Cats

Tigers spend most of their lives living alone. Tigers also hunt alone.

Baby Tigers

Female tigers usually have
two to three babies at a time.
Baby tigers are called **cubs**.

More Facts

- Tigers are excellent swimmers. They can swim several miles at a time.

- A cub will stay with its mother until it is around 2 years old.

- Tigers live around 10 to 15 years in the wild. They can live up to 20 years in captivity.

- There are more tigers captive in the United States than there are tigers in the wild all around the world.

Glossary

cub – a young animal.

grassland – a large area of grass, with little or no trees.

habitat – a place where a living thing is naturally found.

rainforest – a tropical woodland with a lot of rain.

23

Index

abdokids.com

Use this code to log on to abdokids.com and access crafts, games, videos and more!

Abdo Kids Code:
BTK0069